Let me persuade you

1 Look at the range of adjectives below. Circle the ones that could be used to persuade a reader to buy a product.

adorable	average	super
bad	elegant	muddy
expensive	shiny	ugly
fierce	dull	unsightly
attractive	filthy	outstanding
beautiful	horrible	

Write three different sentences you could include in an advert using some of the adjectives you have identified as being persuasive.

1 _____

2 _____

3 _____

2 Write a persuasive advert for the object you chose in the Talk Partner activity on Learner's book page 7. Use the table below to plan your advert.

Create your advert on a separate piece of paper.

Object I am going to advertise	
Adjectives I can use to make my object sound appealing	
Questions I can use in my advert	
Exclamations I can use in my advert	
Statements I can use in my advert	

Report writing

1 Read the following passage and answer the questions below.

> Polar bears are large bears that have white coats.
> They originated from the well-known brown bear.
> They live in the Arctic. Their main source of food is
> ringed seals. They use the ice in the Arctic to sit and
> wait for the seals to come to the surface and breathe.
> When the seal surfaces, the polar bear attacks.

a Where do polar bears originate from?_____

b Where do polar bears live? _____

c What do polar bears eat? _____

2 Summarise each of these sentences using only 10 words.

a Most people think deserts are completely covered by sand but some
are covered in pebbles and rocks or salt where lakes have dried up.

_____

b Other plants grow long roots so that they are able to draw up water
from deep underground.

_____

3 For each set of words, circle the word that is the odd one out in terms
of its suffix.

a helping	hopping	worked	showing
b coped	hoped	helped	shares
c worries	hurries	hurried	scurries

4 Write three words in each column that have the suffix shown,
do not use any of the words from activity 3.

–ing	–ed	–es

A newspaper report

1 Complete each of these sentences to show the key features of newspaper reports:

Use the words to fill in the gaps:

> opinions, headline, past, why, caption, facts, what, where, chronological, quotes

a   Newspaper reports are written in the _____ tense.

b   You can include _____ from people who were at the event being reported.

c   The first paragraph of a newspaper report gives information about who, _____, _____, when and _____.

d   The title at the top of the report is called a _____.

e   The events in the report are written in _____ order to show when they happened.

f   Text written to explain what a photograph is showing is called a _____.

g   The report must contain _____ from your own research.

h   You must leave out your own _____!

2 Read the following newspaper report and label each of the key features of newspapers that are included. Draw arrows and write labels to show that you understand each part of the text.

Farmer united with globetrotting phone

by First News Reporter

A US farmer has been reunited with his phone, after he lost it – and it was shipped to Japan!

Kevin Whitney lost his phone while unloading grain in October last year. The phone, which had fallen into the grain, was then taken on to various boats and vessels before ending up in Japan.

When the boss of a grain company called Mr Whitney to explain they had his phone, he was pretty surprised! The farmer had already purchased a new phone.

The phone was returned to its owner in Oklahoma last month.

Facts and opinions

1 Underline the facts in RED and the opinions in BLUE.

a   Zebras are the most beautiful animals on earth.

b   An adult male lion has a mane.

c   Pirates carried swords.

d   Peacock feathers are prettier than parrots' feathers.

e   Rainbows are formed when the sun is out and it is raining at the same time.

f   Wood comes from trees.

g   Children are always noisy.

2 Use this word bank, as well as your own ideas to write the following sentences:

> **Word bank**
>
> how
> walk
> cheetahs
> shout
> when
> children

a   Two questions

_____

_____

_____

b   Two statements

_____

_____

c   Two orders

_____

_____

_____

_____

Argument texts

1 Look at the following opinions. Sort them into the table below to show whether they are in favour or against the argument for wearing school uniform.

a "School uniform costs too much money, why should I have to buy it for my son?"

b "It would save me having to think about what to wear everyday!"

c "The school pullovers cost less than buying my own pullovers."

d "It would save my favourite clothes from getting covered in pen, paint and mud!"

e "My child is always getting dirty at school – it would mean I would have to do lots more washing every week to make sure they wore clean uniform every day."

f "I don't think all children should have to look the same, they are individuals."

g "I hate the colour blue, why should I be forced to wear a blue pullover to school every day?"

h "I worry too much about what to wear as I don't want to be teased, if we are all wearing the same it would be much better."

Arguments for wearing school uniform	Arguments against wearing school uniform
b,	a,

2 Choose one of the arguments you agree with and write two sentences to explain the point of view. Try to include connectives that structure your argument. For example: *if, although...*

_____

_____

_____

_____

_____

Arguments

1 Circle the adverb in each of these sentences:

a The boy ran to school quickly.

b The cat licked its paws ferociously.

c Children are usually noisy.

d The bull hurtled angrily towards the farmer.

e Unhappily, the man trudged home.

2 This text has no punctuation. Try reading it to yourself. Can you read it fluently?

some people think that children should wear school uniform so they do not get teased by other children because of the clothes they wear they also think it would save time in the mornings as they wouldn't have to decide what to wear many people think it is cheaper to buy uniform than buy designer clothes others think it would be a good idea as their own clothes would not get ruined at school lots of adults think it would help make children feel part of the school and a team as they would all be wearing the same what do you think would you want to wear a school uniform

3 Rewrite the text above, adding in the punctuation required so that you are able to read it fluently and with expression.

_____

_____

_____

_____

_____

_____

_____

_____

Self-assessment

Unit 1

Let's look at non-fiction

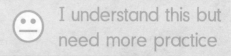 I understand this well

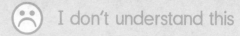 I understand this but need more practice

:(I don't understand this

Learning Objective	:)	:|	:(
Reading			
I can identify questions, statements and orders.			
I can identify adverbs and how they add meaning to a sentence.			
I know how adjectives can be used to make writing persuasive.			
I can identify different types of non-fiction texts.			
I can point out the features of non-fiction texts.			
I can identify key words and phrases in texts.			
I can identify facts and opinions in texts.			
Writing			
I can use a range of end-of-sentence punctuation correctly, e.g. full stops, exclamation marks and question marks.			
I can use connectives to help me structure an argument, e.g. *if, although.*			
I know some common suffixes.			
I can write explanation, persuasive and argument texts.			
I can make notes from a text to summarise key information.			
I can summarise a text into fewer words.			
Speaking and listening			
I can state my viewpoint in an argument.			

I need more help with ...

_____

_____

_____

_____

How are stories put together?

Story openings

1 Match the story opening features/examples to the correct story type, by writing the letter (a–i) in the correct column of the table below.

Features:

a   the reader is told something curious.

b   characters speak to each other.

c   *The stacks of boxes in the dimly lit cave cast dull shadows on the walls.*

d   the reader is introduced to a character straight away.

e   *Rupert, the son of the King, was a naughty boy.*

f   something happens straight away.

g   *Our cat had always appeared normal, that was until I found her talking to my mum.*

h   *"Hello! Would you like to come to my house for lunch?" Robin asked.*

i   The scene is described in detail.

Action	Dialogue	Setting Focus	Character Focus	Narrative Hook

2 Read this story opening.

Maisy and Cho dashed around the corner, pressing themselves hard against the damp wall, wishing it would give way so they could fade with it. Their eyes darted between each other, towards the edge of the wall and then to the corner they had come from. They watched, breathlessly, silently, for any sign of movement, a shadow on the wall, any sign that something was following.

a   What type of opening is it? _____

b   Highlight the text to show the key sentence that identifies the type of opening.

c   How do you know? Give examples from the text in your answer.

_____

_____

More story openings

1 Read the following extracts and write what type of opening it is using the words in the bubble.

dialogue
action
setting focus
character focus
narrative hook

a

"Colin, wake up, you're going to be late again."

"No! Just let me have five more minutes sleep…"

"Five minutes? No chance! You need to leave the house in 10 minutes!"

"Well, I'm going to be late anyway, so five more minutes won't hurt…"

Type of opening

b

The moon shone brightly on the lake as the music came flowing from the house on the shore. The wind rustled the reeds at the lake's edge and the trees stood tall like soldiers ready for battle.

Type of opening

c

The car screeched to a halt. Jake threw open the door, leapt out and ran towards the burning building. Was his family still inside?

Type of opening

d

It wasn't unusual to hear reports about the creature in Lower Westlake. What was peculiar about the latest report was that the creature had been spotted in a house and that it had two heads…

Type of opening

11

Story plans

 Read the following sentences:

a   The wolf tried to catch Little Red Riding hood.

b   The wolf locked Granny in the cupboard.

c   Little Red Riding Hood set off to take cakes to Granny.

d   The woodcutter rescued Granny and Little Red Riding Hood.

e   The wolf put on Granny's clothes and sat in bed.

f   She met a wolf and told him where she was going.

g   Little Red Riding Hood knocked on the door of Granny's house.

h   The woodcutter heard Little Red Riding Hood's screams.

i   The wolf ran ahead to get to Granny's before Little Red-Riding Hood.

Sort them by writing the letter (a – i) into the story plan below to show which part of the story they come from:

Climax

Build-up	Events leading to end

Introduction	Conclusion

 For each example shown, circle the verb and identify the tense of the sentence. Write your own sentence using the same verb and tense as the example.

a   She was scared of wolves for evermore.

_____

b   We had a party to celebrate the end of the wolf!

_____

c   You will have to look out for more wolves in the wood.

_____

d   She is happy to be home safely.

_____

e   "I will be careful not to talk to wolves in the future," said Little Red Riding Hood

_____

Genre and story endings

1 Match the statements to the correct genre

Includes strange happenings and usually a detective of some kind who solves a puzzle or crime.
Stories that have the basis in events that happened in the past.
Stories about technology of the future or from another world. Often set in space.
Elements that are not realistic, e.g. talking animals, set in other universe, mythical beings.
Contain lots of fast-paced action and involve danger, risk and excitement.

Fantasy
Mystery
Adventure
Science Fiction
Historical

2 Fill in the missing punctuation in this story ending.

would anyone ever find their beloved Pompeii they wondered would anyone ever see its splendid streets perhaps perhaps not

tranio and livia walked back to their small house beside the orange grove for the rest of their days they would carry a deep sorrow within their hearts

3 Read the story ending above, as well as the other extracts from 'Escape from Pompeii' on page 29 of the Learner's Book, and answer the following questions:

a Where do you think Pompeii had gone? Why do you think this?

_____

b Had Tranio and Livia liked living in Pompeii? How do you know?

_____

c What was the 'deep sorrow' they would carry in their hearts forever?

_____

Story planning and feedback

1 Look at these story stages. For each box, give it a heading to show which part of the story it is from. Number each box to show the order they would go in to tell the story.

> beginning, build-up, climax, resolution, ending

Sleeping Beauty finds a spinning wheel. Pricks her finger. Whole castle sleeps for 100 years.	Sleeping Beauty and Prince marry and they all live happily ever after. Bad fairy is punished.	Sleeping Beauty is born. All invited to party to celebrate. One fairy is not invited.	Prince finds castle through overgrown hedges. Kisses Sleeping Beauty and whole castle wakes.	Party. Bad fairy arrives and says Sleeping Beauty will die when pricked with a spinning wheel needle. Good fairy changes so she won't die but sleep for 100 years.

2 Write the beginning of the story using the notes above to help you.

_____

_____

_____

_____

_____

_____

Tenses

1 Change these sentences into past tense.

    a   I play football in the park.

    _____

    b   I will work hard during the test.

    _____

    c   I will sing on the stage.

    _____

    d   I eat my lunch every day at 12 o'clock.

    _____

2 Rewrite these sentences so that the verb tenses are correct:

    a   I sang on the stage tomorrow.

    _____

    b   Yesterday, I will ride my bike to school.

    _____

    c   I am sang in the choir now.

    _____

    d   Tomorrow it was my birthday!

    _____

3 Change these sentences into present tense.

    a   I walked to school.

    _____

    b   I drove a car.

    _____

    c   I watched television.

    _____

    d   I ran to the shops.

    _____

Adjectives

1 Write adjectives around each of these pictures to describe them.

2 For each picture, write a sentence that includes a verb, adjective and adverb. Use a separate piece of paper for your writing.

Self-assessment

Unit 2

How are stories put together?

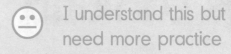

☺ I understand this well

😐 I understand this but need more practice

☹ I don't understand this

Learning Objective	☺	😐	☹
Reading			
I can identify adverbs and understand their impact.			
I understand the five main stages in a story.			
I can retell events from a text to answer questions.			
I can use punctuation marks to read with expression.			
Writing			
I can use more powerful verbs in my writing.			
I understand the past, present and future tenses of verbs.			
I can explore different openings and endings of stories.			
I am beginning to use paragraphs to organise my stories.			
Speaking and listening			
I can listen carefully during discussions as well as giving my own ideas.			

I need more help with ...

_____

_____

_____

_____

Unit 3 Looking at poetry

Haikus

1 Write a haiku. First, create a mind map for an object. Write the object in the box below. Then write words and phrases around the edge of the box to describe it. *(e.g. What does it look like? How does it feel? What is it made of?)* Include some ideas for imagery using figurative language such as similes.

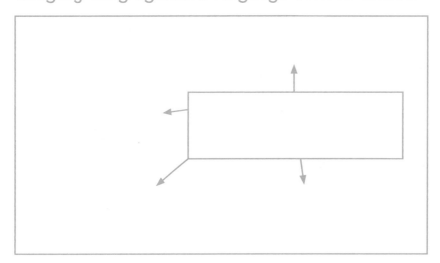

Glossary

Imagery: language that describes what something looks like and gives the reader an image in their heads.

Figurative language: language that uses words or expressions that are different from the literal meaning – it helps the reader to infer different meaning from the words.

Simile: when something is described by comparing it with something else using the words 'as' or 'like'.

2 Use the words from the mind map to write your haiku below. Remember:

- The poem is three lines long.
- The first line contains 5 syllables.
- The second line contains 7 syllables.
- The last line contains 5 syllables.

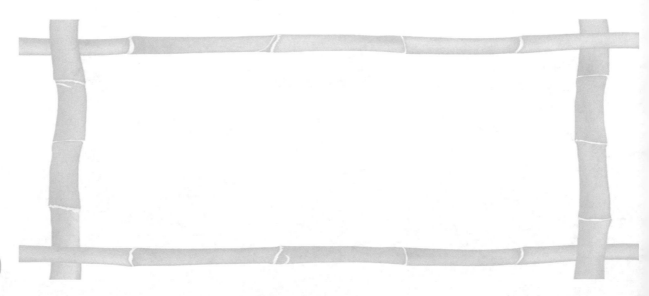

Creating mood

Listen

Shhhhhhhhhhhhh!
Sit still, very still
And listen.
Listen to wings
Lighter than eyelashes
Stroking the air.
Know that the thin breeze
Whispers on high
To the coconut trees.
Listen and hear.

By Telcine Turner

1 Read the poem by Telcine Turner and answer these questions:

a   Write down the creature described in the poem._____

b   What part of the creature sounds 'lighter than eyelashes'? _____

c   Why is this part of the creature described as 'stroking the air'?
_____
_____

d   What is making the sound in the coconut trees?
_____

e   What does the poet mean by the '*thin breeze whispers on high to the coconut trees*'?
_____
_____

f   Identify a powerful verb in the poem and explain why you have chosen it.
_____

g   What is the setting for the poem? Is this shown explicitly or implicitly? Explain your answer. _____
_____

h   Read the poem again. Now what you know what the poem is about, explain why you think the poet chose *Shhhhhhhhhhhhh!* to start the poem.
_____
_____

Older poetry

Humming Bird

I can imagine, in some otherworld
Primeval-dumb, far back
In that most awful stillness, that only gasped and hummed,
Humming-birds raced down the avenues.

Before anything had a soul,
While life was a heave of Matter, half inanimate,
This little bit chipped off in brilliance
And went whizzing through the slow, vast, succulent stems.

I believe there were no flowers, then,
In the world where the humming-bird flashed ahead of creation.
I believe he pierced the slow vegetable veins with his long beak.

Probably he was big
As mosses, and little lizards, they say were once big.
Probably he was a jabbing, terrifying monster.
We look at him through the wrong end of the long telescope of Time,
Luckily for us.

By D.H. Lawrence

1 Read the poem by D.H. Lawrence. There are tricky words in the poem as it was written a long time ago and contains some older language.

2 Match the word from the poem to its meaning.
You can use a dictionary to help you.

primeval	shows no signs of life
avenues	tender, juicy and tasty
inanimate	earliest time in history
chipped	an instrument to make objects far away appear nearer
pierced	a broad road in a town or city that is lined with trees
telescope	force a way through or go in to
succulent	cut or break

Lifecycle poems

1 Use the pictures to write a short poem about the life cycle of a chicken based on the poem *Lifecycle of a butterfly* below. Do not worry about making your poem rhyme. Plan some ideas for your poem first:

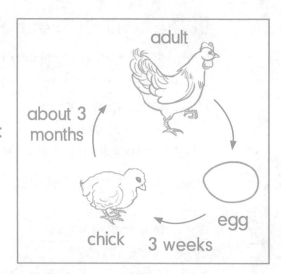

a   Write some words to show how a chicken moves, for example, on two legs, head still, small-steps …

b   Write some possible places where a chicken may make a nest, for example, in a shed, in straw, in a box…

c   Make a list of predators for a chicken to help you with the last few lines, for example foxes, hawks…

a _____

b _____

c _____

(use ideas from b) ⎤

(use ideas from a) ⎤

Lifecycle of a butterfly	Lifecycle of a chicken
Brown and furry	Brown and feathery
Caterpillar in a hurry,	Chicken _____
Take your walk	Lay your egg
To the shady leaf, or stalk,	_____
Or what not,	Or what not,
Which may be the chosen spot.	Which may be the chosen spot.
No toad spy you,	No _____ spy you
Hovering bird of prey pass by you;	_____ pass by you
Spin and die,	Crack open from the egg
To live again a butterfly.	To be a newborn chick.

By Christina Rossetti

(use ideas from c)

Funny poems

In The Land Of The Bumbley Boo

In the land of the Bumbley Boo
The People are red white and blue,
They never blow noses,
Or ever wear closes,
What a sensible thing to do!

In the land of the Bumbley Boo
You can buy Lemon pie at the zoo;
They give away foxes
In little Pink Boxes
And Bottles of Dandylion Stew.

In the land of the Bumbley Boo
You never see a Gnu,
But thousands of cats
Wearing trousers and hats
Made of Pumpkins and Pelican Glue!

Chorus
Oh, the Bumbley Boo! the Bumbley Boo!
That's the place for me and you!
So hurry! Let's run!
The train leaves at one!
For the land of the Bumbley Boo!
The wonderful Bumbley Boo-Boo-Boo!
The Wonderful Bumbley BOO!!!

By Spike Milligan

1 Read the poem in your head. Which part is your favourite and why?

_____

2 What does the poet mean by the word 'closes' in the first verse?
How do you know? Why has he written it like this?

_____

3 What do you think makes this poem funny? Think about the rhyming
structure, the images created and overall theme when writing your answer.

_____

Self-assessment
Unit 3
Looking at poetry

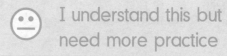

	😊 I understand this well
😐	I understand this but need more practice
☹️	I don't understand this

Learning Objective	😊	😐	☹️
Reading			
I can identify powerful verbs in a poem.			
I can spot the rhyming patterns in a poem.			
I know a variety of reading strategies to help me tackle unfamiliar words.			
I can use punctuation to help me read aloud with expression.			
I can point out an implicit meaning in a poem.			
I can point out an explicit meaning in a poem.			
I know what figurative language means.			
Writing			
I can use powerful verbs when writing poetry.			
I can use similes when writing poetry.			
Speaking and listening			
I can comment on the way a poem is read.			

I need more help with ...

_____

_____

_____

_____

23

 Let's persuade!

Unit 4

Features of adverts

1 Match the definition to the example sentence.

Play on words	Racing raisins
Alliteration	Are you bored of the same old snack?
Rhetorical questions	Try our new snack pack raisins!
Hook	These are hair raisin'!

2 Find the pairs of homophones in the wordsearch puzzle

Homophones

t	h	g	i	n	k	y	r	x	n	a	h
m	m	r	f	d	f	v	z	u	n	u	a
b	e	a	r	l	i	a	s	i	o	p	r
a	u	e	o	h	p	m	s	r	l	l	e
c	g	w	t	h	y	f	i	f	g	v	f
e	e	z	h	j	a	I	l	e	d	i	o
r	l	l	g	c	e	i	e	d	c	n	l
j	c	n	i	s	a	e	r	h	w	a	o
p	i	y	n	z	r	v	m	w	d	t	r
a	e	e	s	a	x	d	l	b	n	m	g
o	y	q	b	q	m	z	d	a	t	e	v
e	k	n	g	s	t	t	z	s	i	m	o

bare
bear
eye
I
flour
flower
hair
hare
knight
night

3 Match the definitions to the correct homophone

bare	A white powder created by grinding wheat
bear	The organs that we see through
eye	A fast-running long eared mammal
I	The time from sunset to sunrise
flour	The personal pronoun
flower	Fine thread-like strands found on skin
hair	not covered
hare	The part of a plant that bears seeds
knight	A hairy mammal with a large body
night	A man from the middle ages who wore armour

Leaflets

GET SNAPPY AT **ALLIGATOR ISLE**

Visit Alligator Isle for a once-in-a-lifetime experience! First, you will have an aerial adventure on the island. Then you will take to the water in our specially adapted boats, ensuring a safe, close-up encounter with the alligators.

This year sees the introduction of our new and exciting ALLIGATOR NURSERY, where you can admire and hold baby alligators. Have your camera ready to snap those snappy fellas!

Can you afford to miss out on the fun? Come to the place where amazing alligator-memories are made!

The best day ever – I even held an alligator!

Simone (aged 8)

Jenson (aged 13)

The aerial adventure was AMAZING – you could see the whole island from one window!

Book online and save money.
Visit our website for more information.
www.isleofalligators.com

 1

Use a different colour to underline the following features on the leaflet. Complete the key below to show which colour matches each feature.

KEY

COLOUR	FEATURE
	A clear heading
	Photograph of the attraction
	Review from a previous visitor
	Key information
	A fact about the attraction
	An opinion about the attraction
	A rhetorical question
	A feature designed to attract previous visitors to the attraction
	An example of a play on words
	An explicit meaning
	An implicit meaning

Adverts

1 Look at these different sentence types:

> Statement, Fact, Question, Opinion, Order

For each of these sentences (taken from leaflets/adverts) identify the type of sentence it is and write in the box.

a   Bored on the school holidays? [ ]

b   The food was amazing! [ ]

c   Book your tickets now. [ ]

d   The park opens on 1st April every year. [ ]

e   Home of the BIG zoo animals. [ ]

f   Wetlands are amazing! [ ]

g   Check out our facebook page. [ ]

h   Are you up for the challenge? [ ]

2 Plan an advertising poster for an attraction of your choice. Use this planning frame to help you. Use more paper if you need to.

Layout and presentation features to include: (write your ideas next to each heading)		Text features to include: (write your ideas next to each heading)	
Clear, bold heading		Rhetorical question	
Special offers		Play on words	
Captions for photos		A fact	
How will quotes be presented?		Key details	
What colours will you use?		Quotes	

My advert

1 Draw your poster here.

Non-fiction texts

1 Complete the sentences using the words from this word bank:

a _____ texts try to _____ the reader to a particular point of view.

b _____ texts tell the reader about a process in detail.

c _____ reports often contain _____ from observers.

d _____ texts consist of a series of _____ related to a particular event or subject.

e Explanation texts often have a labelled _____ to explain the text.

f Two examples of persuasive texts are _____ and _____.

g Newspaper reports are written in _____.

> **Word bank**
>
> quotes
> Explanation
> adverts
> Persuasive
> leaflets
> convince
> paragraphs
> diagram
> Newspaper
> Report
> columns

2 For each of the text types below, circle the feature that is **the odd one out** (not related to the text type).

LEAFLETS	conclusion	bright colours	bold headings
NEWSPAPERS	written in columns	quotes	address at top
EXPLANATIONS	opening paragraph	headlines	labelled diagrams
ADVERTS	rhetorical questions	bold colours	headlines
LETTERS	labelled diagram	address at top	who it is to

Overused words

1 Read this newspaper report and underline the overused (repeated) words. Use a thesaurus to find different words that make sense. Cross out the words you are replacing and write your new words above them.

FASCINATING FACTS

Today saw the opening of a new dinosaur museum 'DINO-WORLD' for the city of Kochi. The mayor of the city was there to cut the ribbon and declare the new visitor attraction open. Local schoolchildren were among the first guests to surge forward and enter the new building.

The curator of the museum said, "We are really thrilled to see so much enthusiasm! Today is the climax of many years of planning and we are really delighted the museum is finally open!"

The museum houses a really big collection of life-size dinosaur models, dinosaur skeletons and stories of other really big prehistoric animals that roamed the earth many millions of years ago. It includes many hands-on experiences, including brass rubbings of dinosaur footprints, a moving Tyrannosaurus Rex, fossil-hunting and many more!

With a really well stocked gift shop and café, the reaction of visitors was a really big thumbs up. Mariyah, aged 9 said, "This is the best museum I have ever been to, I really want to come every weekend!"

Key features of a non-fiction text

1 All of the clues relate to a particular type of non-fiction text.

What type of text is it? _____

How do you know this? _____

ACROSS

2 One of the Ws
5 One of the Ws
6 One of the Ws
7 Things that people have said about the event
8 The title at the top of the report
9 Captions are used to explain what these are

DOWN

1 The person who wrote the report
3 The way this type of text is laid out
4 Information about a photograph
5 One of the Ws
6 One of the Ws

Table mountain in South Africa

Self-assessment

Unit 4

Let's persuade!

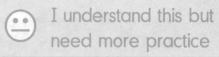	I understand this well		
	I understand this but need more practice		
	I don't understand this		

Learning Objective	🙂	😐	☹️
Reading			
I can apply my phonic and spelling knowledge to read unfamiliar words.			
I can understand the use of connectives to structure an argument.			
I can identify different types of non-fiction texts and know their key features.			
I can understand how persuasive texts are used to convince readers.			
I can identify facts and opinions in texts.			
Writing			
I can find different words to replace overused ones.			
I can explore the layout and presentation of writing and understand how this helps the purpose of the text.			
Speaking and listening			
I can deal politely with views that are different from my own.			

I need more help with ...

_____

_____

_____

_____

Unit 5 Story settings and characters

Character details

Harry looked at the bird, which had now stopped at the edge of the table and was standing, looking up at him, its head cocked to one side. All he could think of was what a large sharp beak it had and what cruel curved talons on its scaly feet. He shut his eyes tight, and put his hand on the table top.

"Hullo, Madison," he gulped nervously.

Very gently, the parrot stepped on to Harry's arm. Very gently, it climbed slowly up and perched on his shoulder. Very gently, it nibbled at the lobe of his ear.

Harry opened his eyes, and a grin of relief spread over his face.

1 Read the character description above and answer the following questions:

a Find and copy the phrase that shows what Harry thought Madison's talons were. _____

b How does Harry feel at the end? How do you know?

_____

c Why does Harry change his opinion of Madison during this description?

_____

2 Sort the statements below into the correct box in the table to show implicit and explicit details about each of the characters.

Key explicit details	Key implicit details

a Harry is a boy

b Harry thinks the parrot is going to bite him.

c Madison has a sharp beak.

d Madison is a parrot.

e The parrot is friendly.

f Harry is afraid of holding the parrot.

Words characters say

1 Choose a character from a book you have read recently. Make notes about the character using the table below. Think carefully about each part to make your character as detailed as possible.

My character's name: _____

My character is from this book_____

Appearance (what the character looks like)	
Personality (the type of character they are, e.g. happy or shy)	
Likes (things/people/food the character likes)	
Dislikes (things/people/food the character dislikes)	

2 Write three sentences to show three things that your character might say. Remember to use speech marks in your sentences.

For example: "I love spending time with my friends, especially when we are shopping!"

1 _____

2 _____

3 _____

Character traits

Complete the crossword using the clues to discover the character's name.

Across

3   He is very tall and lives at the top of a beanstalk.

6   He has a shell and walks very slowly.

8   He likes living under a bridge and scaring goats!

9   He likes to boast about being the fastest animal.

10   He likes climbing tall plants.

11   He is as thin as a pencil.

Down

1   He doesn't want to be eaten so runs away.

2   He likes to eat porridge for breakfast.

4   She likes to look after her granny.

5   He likes to eat three boiled chickens for breakfast.

7   She likes sleeping in small, cosy beds.

Planning a setting

They were looking down upon a lovely valley.
There were green meadows on either side of
the valley, and along the bottom of it there
flowed a great brown river.

What is more, there was a tremendous waterfall
halfway along the river – a steep cliff over which
the water curled and rolled in a solid sheet, and
then went crashing down into a boiling churning
whirlpool of froth and spray.

1 Read the setting description above and answer the following questions:

    a   What colour was the river at the bottom of the valley? _____

    b   What was halfway along the river? _____

    c   Find and write three powerful verbs used in the description.

       _____

    d   Find and write three adjectives used in the description.

       _____

2 Underline words and phrases describing what the scene looks or sounds like above that help you build the picture in your head.

3 The setting description above is taken from Charlie and the Chocolate Factory by Roald Dahl. The scene described is made from sweets and the river is flowing chocolate. Re-read the description. How does this knowledge change how you picture the scene in your head?

_____

_____

4 For each sentence below, write **I** if it is an implicit detail or **E** if it explicit in the text.

    a   The people looking at the scene were standing above it. _____

    b   The water from the waterfall crashed into a whirlpool. _____

    c   The waterfall was noisy. _____

    d   The people liked the scene they were looking at. _____

Powerful verbs

The man walked slowly towards his house. He nudged a can with his foot. It went down the street. He turned into his driveway. His feet walked on the gravel. He turned the key in the lock on his door. A little boy walked up to him and hugged him. The man smiled. The boy laughed.

1 Read the text above and write the verbs used in the table below. Next write an alternative for each verb so that it becomes a more interesting, powerful verb.

Verbs in the text	Alternatives (more powerful verbs)

2 Using your ideas from the table rewrite the text, replacing the verbs with more powerful ones. Remember to check your writing still makes sense.

_____

_____

_____

_____

_____

3 For each sentence below, underline the adverb and then rewrite the sentence using an adverb that creates a contrast to the original sentence.
For example: The man walked <u>slowly</u> towards his house.
The man walked <u>quickly</u> towards his house.

a   He nudged a can hard with his foot.

_____

b   He turned hastily into his driveway.

_____

c   His feet walked loudly on the gravel.

_____

Homophones

1 For the following homophones, use a dictionary to write the alternatives for each. Write the definition for each word underneath each.

e.g.	to	two	too
	preposition – expressing motion	a number – equivalent to the sum of one and one	adverb – in addition or a higher degree than is desirable

a	through	

b	ate	

c	red	

d	sea	

e	their	

f	sail	

2 Complete these sentences using the correct homophone from above:

a I wanted to _____ the view for myself.

b We went to the shops early so we could buy things in the _____.

c I _____ three books yesterday.

d The food was tasty so I _____ it all up!

e I _____ the ball for my dog to fetch.

f It was _____ turn to have a go on the swings.

Summarising details

Not far from where I live there is a queer old empty wooden house standing all by itself on the side of the road. I long to explore inside it but the door is always locked, and when I peer through a window all I can see is darkness and dust. I know the ground floor used once to be a shop because I can still read the faded lettering across the front which says THE GRUBBER. My mother has told me that in our part of the country in the olden days a grubber was another name for a sweet-shop, and now everytime I look at it I think to myself what a lovely old sweet-shop it must have been.

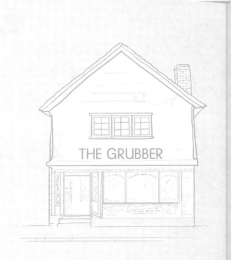

THE GRUBBER

1 Read the setting description above and write phrases from it into the table to show the features listed in the table.

Explicit details	*For example: The house must have been empty for a very long time.*
Implicit details	*For example: The ground floor used to be a sweet shop.*
What mood is created?	
Powerful verbs used	
Adverbs used	
What details do you find out about the narrator?	

2 Read the setting description above and answer the following questions:

a How does the narrator know the ground floor used to be a shop?

_____

b How does the author know what a Grubber is?

_____

c What word that shows the narrator really wants to explore the house?

_____

Self-assessment

Unit 5

Story settings and characters

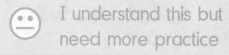

😊 I understand this well

😐 I understand this but need more practice

☹ I don't understand this

Learning Objective	😊	😐	☹
Reading			
I understand how settings and characters are built up through details in the text.			
I understand the difference between explicit and implicit meaning in texts.			
I understand how language can be used to create mood.			
Writing			
I can understand the meaning of homophones.			
I can use the apostrophe to show possession.			
I can use speech marks correctly.			
I have identified different ways of planning stories.			
I can choose and compare words to improve my writing.			
I can write character profiles.			
Speaking and listening			
I can adapt my speech and movements to play a character in drama.			

I need more help with ...

_____

_____

_____

_____

Let's act!

Playscript features

Read the playscript below. Find an example of each feature in the text and circle it in a colour. Use a different colour for each feature. Then complete the key below using the colours you have chosen for each feature.

CAST:

Teacher	Ling
Annabel	Anika
Marcus	Sebastian

Hometime

Scene I: *A classroom with individual desks*

Teacher: Thank you for working so hard today, (*turning to Anika*) all except Anika… The rest of you may get your coats and go home.

Children: (*moving towards classroom door and chatting to one another*) Bye!

Anika: (*looking sullen*) But it wasn't my fault, Miss… I was just trying to tell Ling that she was wrong. She got cross.

Teacher: (*calmly*) I understand what happened. I know you were trying to help but you need to take more care with the way that you say things. People don't like it when you just tell them they are wrong. You need to explain why you think that. People are allowed different opinions.

Anika: (*thoughtfully*) I s'pose so…

Teacher: (*laughing*) I know so! Now next time things go wrong, instead of sulking, try to think about what you can do to make it better.

Anika: (*standing up*) Thank you, I will. Bye.

KEY

COLOUR	FEATURE OF PLAYSCRIPT
	A title
	Character list
	A scene with clear information about what the setting looks like
	Characters' names on the left with colons after them to show what they say.
	New lines for each new speaker
	Stage directions written in the present tense

Narrative order

1 Create a scene list of a new playscript! Write the scene heading, a list of the characters and a short sentence describing the main action that occurs. For example:

Scene 1: *A castle in Peru.*
Character: *Prince Alfredo and his mother*
Action: *Alfredo and his mother have an argument.*

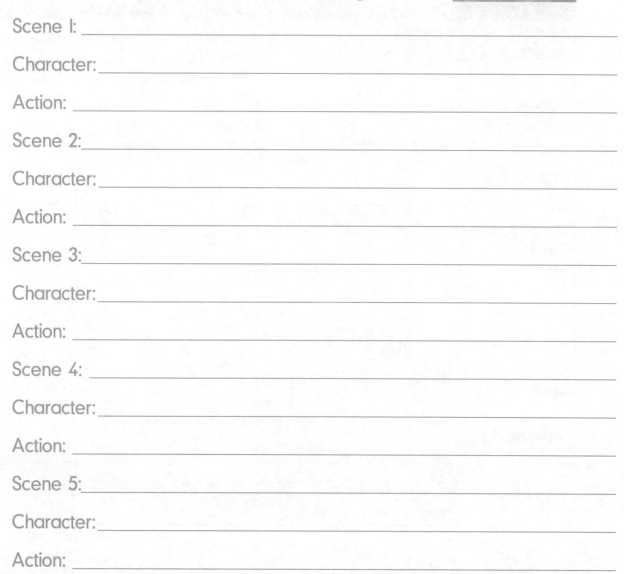

Scene 1: _____

Character: _____

Action: _____

Scene 2: _____

Character: _____

Action: _____

Scene 3: _____

Character: _____

Action: _____

Scene 4: _____

Character: _____

Action: _____

Scene 5: _____

Character: _____

Action: _____

2 Now choose one scene and write it in full on a separate piece of paper.

Stage directions

1 For each of the stage directions below, tick to show whether it is setting the scene, telling the character what to do or telling the character how to speak. Add three of your own at the bottom and tick to show which type of stage direction they are.

Stage direction	Setting the scene	Telling characters what to do	Telling characters how to speak
quietly			
A cottage in the woods			
carrying a torch			
backing out of the room			
Moving towards the house			
A stream, with a bridge and a troll underneath			
whispering			
shouting			

More stage directions

Scene: A kitchen. An old woman is opening the oven to take out a tray with a gingerbread man on.

Old woman: (_____)
I'm very pleased with him! I can't wait to eat the tasty gingerbread
(_____ !)

Gingerbread man leaps up from the (_____) *and runs to the door.*

Gingerbread man: (_____)
But I don't want to be eaten. You'll have to
(_____) me first.

Gingerbread man:(_____).

Old woman: (_____) STOP! STOP!

Gingerbread man: (*singing*) Run! Run! As fast as you
(_____), you can't catch me I'm the
(_____) man!

1 Fill in the missing words in the playscript using the words from the Word bank:

2 Write the missing stage directions of the play into the brackets.

3 Highlight the stage directions in three colours: setting the scene (red), telling the character what to do (blue), telling the character how to speak (yellow).

Word bank

Gingerbread
tray
biscuit
can
catch

Playscripts

Solve the clues to complete the crossword.

Across

5 The people that play the parts in a play
6 Stage directions are written in this way to make them look different
7 There are a number of these in a play and they change whent he action changes
8 Instructions that tell the actors what to do
9 The words that tell the actor what to say and do for the whole play

Down

1. The moveable objects on stage
2. The clothes that are worn by the people performing the play
3 The fictional people in the play
4 Where the action takes place

Self-assessment

Unit 6

Let's act!

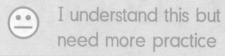 I understand this well

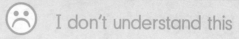 I understand this but need more practice

I don't understand this

Learning Objective	🙂	😐	☹
Reading			
I can use my knowledge of punctuation and grammar to read fluently and with expression.			
I can read and perform playscripts.			
I can explore narrative order and identify key events.			
I can investigate how settings and characters are built up from details in the text.			
Writing			
I can elaborate on basic information with some detail.			
Speaking and listening			
I can adapt my speech and gestures to create a character in drama.			
I listen carefully in discussions and contribute my own ideas as well.			

I need more help with ...

_____

_____

_____

_____

Unit 7 Looking at fiction

Story stages

1 Fill in the missing words in each sentence using this word bank:

Word bank

stages
build-up
climax
narrative order
introduction
significant
resolution

a The _____ is the very first stage in the story.

b _____ events are the most important events that happen in the story.

c The events that happen before the main part of the story are known as the _____.

d The most important part of the story that happens in the middle is called the _____.

e The _____ is where everything is sorted out before the story ends.

f There are five main _____ in every story.

g The events in stories are written in _____ so that the reader understands what is happening and how events are related.

2 Use the words from the word bank above and fit them into the crossword puzzle. Look carefully at the number of letters in each word to help you.

Significant events

Goat Escape!

The zookeeper fed the animals, made sure they had enough water for the night and then locked the sheds. He was tired after his busy day looking after all the animals in the Petting Zoo.

As he put his coat on he thought that he had forgotten something but he couldn't think what it was and anyway, he was looking forward to his dinner that was waiting for him at home.

He had forgotten to close the goat's gate …

The goats had a wonderful time exploring the zoo at night. They ate all sorts of things that they shouldn't … bins, fences, grass in the rabbit's enclosure, the zoo keeper's boots … and much, much more.

The next morning, the zookeeper was still wondering about what he had forgotten when suddenly he remembered … the goats! He followed the trail and found the goats curled up and sleeping in the rabbit enclosure. He quickly herded them back to their enclosure and set about tidying up the mess!

1 Underline the significant events in the story above.

2 Complete this plan to show the narrative order of the story by writing the significant events in the table.

Story stage	Significant events
Beginning	
Events leading to climax	
Climax (most significant event)	
Events leading to end	
Conclusion	

Apostrophes for possession

1 Create a sentence using an apostrophe to show possession using words from the word bank below. An example has been done for you. Complete four different sentences.

Rachel	boy	coat	tail
children	Chen	book	bone
lady	dog	milk	dress
Tom	man	pegs	bag
lion	horses	room	painting
men	Chris	mane	toy
girl	cat	umbrella	house

Rachel got the boy's coat.

a _____

b _____

c _____

d _____

2 Correct these sentences by adding the apostrophe to show possession.

a It was Marks turn to play the game.

b The girls coats were hanging on their pegs.

c Daniellas painting won the prize.

d After school, they all went to Sams house.

3 Rewrite these sentences using apostrophes for omission where necessary. The first one has been done for you.

a I will have to learn my spelling.   <u>I'll have to learn my spelling.</u>

b It was not her turn to play.

_____

c I can not play tonight.

_____

d I will not be able to come to the party.

_____

Intensity of adjectives

1 Add adjectives to the spaces below to show the change in intensity of this adjective. Use a thesaurus to help you.

a cold (_____) warm (_____) hot (_____) scorching

⟵——————————————————————————————————⟶

b bright (_____) vivid (_____) dazzling

⟵——————————————————————————————————⟶

2 Using the words above from activity 1 a, write three sentences using a different adjective in each to change the intensity of the description. For example, *The water in the bath was tepid.*

a _____

b _____

c _____

3 Using the words above from activity 1 b, write three sentences using a different adjective in each to change the intensity of the description. For example, *The bright light shone on the water.*

a _____

_____

b _____

c _____

4 Put this list of adjectives in order to show the change in intensity.

(vicious   unkind   cruel   hurtful   disagreeable)

_____

_____

Settings

The Beach

The sand glistened like gold. The sea sparkled like diamonds. People laughed, joked and ran around playing games on the beach and in the sea. The white-brick lifeguard tower stood proud on the rocks. The gulls circled above, calling to one another when food was dropped. Ice-cream vans and fish-and-chip shops lined the promenade, enticing people to try their offerings. Colourful windbreaks broke up the golden sand, creating small camps for the armies of people.

1 Read the setting description above and fill in the table to show the things that you would hear, feel and smell if you were standing in the scene. Divide your answers into things that are explicit (shown in the text) and implicit (things that you infer from the text).

	Explicit details (details in the text)	Implicit details (details I can infer from the text)
Sights	e.g. the golden sand	*The sun must be shining as the sea is glistening.*
Sounds		
Feelings		
Smells		

2 Underline the similes that are used in the description above.

3 Read the text again and answer the following questions:

a Why did the gulls call to one another? _____

b What was the lifeguard tower made from? _____

c From the description, explain what a promenade is. _____

_____

Character profiles

Perhaps it had something to do with living in a dark cupboard, but Harry had always been small and skinny for his age. He looked even smaller and skinnier that he really was because all he had to wear were old clothes of Dudley's and Dudley was about four times bigger than he was. Harry had a thin face, knobbly knees, black hair and bright green eyes. He wore round glasses held together with a lot of sellotape because of all the times Dudley had punched him in the nose. The only thing Harry liked about his appearance was a very thin scar on his forehead which was shaped like a bolt of lightning.

1 Read the character description above and complete the following table to show details about the character. Divide your answers into explicit details and implicit details.

Feature	Explicit details	Implicit details
Name		
Age		
Looks		
Clothes		
Personality		

2 Use the table above to draw a picture of the character in the description above. Add labels to your drawing to show the key details, e.g. what age is the character? What do they like doing?

Character description

 Use this Word bank to write a character description. Some of the details will come from the words given, others will come from your imagination:

Before writing, plan your description carefully:

- What does your character look like?
- What personality does your character have?
- What information do you want your reader to infer about the character?
- What information will you tell your reader (explicit details)?

> REMEMBER! Use adjectives and similes to make your description entertaining and detailed.

Word bank

friendly
adventurous
brave blonde
boy freckles
young
thoughtful
keen

_____

_____

_____

_____

_____

_____

_____

_____

_____

_____

_____

_____

_____

Self-assessment
Unit 7
Looking at fiction

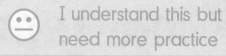

☺	I understand this well	
😐	I understand this but need more practice	
☹	I don't understand this	

Learning Objective	☺	😐	☹
Reading			
I can explore narrative order and identify key events.			
I understand the main stages in a story.			
I can give a personal response to a text.			
Writing			
I can identify syllabic patterns in longer words.			
I understand that adjectives have different degrees of intensity.			
I can use an apostrophe to show possession.			
I can use commas to show meaning in sentences.			
I am beginning to use paragraphs to organise and sequence my ideas.			
Speaking and listening			
I can adapt my speech and gestures to create a character in drama.			

I need more help with ...

_____

_____

_____

_____

_____

Unit 8 Changing stories into reports

Key words and phrases

Re-read these paragraphs from the story in the Learner's Book:

"What was that?" Mateo twisted his head quickly in the direction of the sound that had come from the bushes. He stalked closer, treading carefully on the forest floor. He could hear a faint rustling from under the bush.

Lifting the lower branches carefully, Mateo peered into the space below the bush. There, huddled up in a small ball, was a small, furry creature. Two pairs of large, round eyes stared up at him. Slowly, the creature unfurled two large, bat-like ears, which it waggled playfully. Mateo reached down and put a hand out. The creature lifted itself onto a pair of stubby legs, which ended in two small pink feet. As it raised itself, Mateo noticed that it seemed to have two more pairs of legs, which it used to steady itself. Mateo gaped.

1

   a   What did Mateo have to lift to see the creature? _____

   b   Find and write a **question** Mateo asks. _____

   c   How many legs does the creature have? _____

   d   Draw a picture of the creature in the story. Add labels to show the features of the creature using the description from the text above.

2   Match the parts from the story to the correct story stage by drawing lines.

Beginning	There, huddled up in a small ball, was a small, furry creature
Build-up	"Do you want to come home with me?"
Climax	"What was that?"
Events leading to resolution	"I'm going to be famous!"
Resolution	Slowly, carefully he reached down and stroked the little animal.

Features of newspapers

1 Sort these words and phrases into the correct paragraph in this plan.

> further details about the event or story / name of people involved / quotes from people involved / what happened / where the event happened / what has happened as a result of the event or story / when it happened / why it is being reported / future projects from the event or story

Orientation paragraph	
Main story paragraph	
Re-orientation paragraph	

2 For each of the headlines below, write what type of headline it is.

a   New planet discovered? _____

b   Teacher achieves great results! _____

c   "New hope for patients" says leading doctor. _____

3 Write your own suitable headlines for the following stories. Try to vary the type of headline you use for each one.

a   A boy has broken the world record for highest trampoline bounce.

_____

b   A cat was stuck at the top of a tree and had to be rescued by firefighters.

_____

Comprehension

Read the beginning of this newspaper report (related to the story paragraphs you read on page 54):

New Creature similar to a cat?

Last night, Mateo Aguas (aged 10) found an amazing creature in the woods at the bottom of his garden. Scientists have yet to name the creature, but they have confirmed that it has never been seen before.

Mateo Aguas was a normal boy until last night, when he made a discovery that is sure to make him famous. He was out walking in the woods at the bottom of his garden, when he heard a noise, which caused him to stop.

"It was weird," Mateo told our reporter, "It was like nothing I've ever seen before. It was like something from a movie!"

1

a   What type of headline has been used?

_____

b   Who did Mateo say 'It was weird' to?

_____

c   How many (and which) of the five Ws is mentioned in the orientation paragraph?

_____

d   Why is Mateo no longer a 'normal' boy? What do you think will happen to him after the discovery?

_____

_____

2   Write an alternative headline for the newspaper story above using a different headline technique than the one already used.

_____

Connectives

1 Sort the following connectives in to the correct column of the table to show whether they are **co-ordinating** or **subordinating**.

if   although   and   but   because   when   so   or   while   since

Co-ordinating connectives	Sub-ordinating connectives
to join two clauses independent and of equal importance to one other	*link a main clause with a dependent clause*

2 Complete these sentences using one of the connectives from the table above. Think carefully about whether it needs to be a co-ordinating or sub-ordinating connective.

a   I did not feel well last week, _____ still went to school.

b   Help yourself to anything you can find, _____ you feel hungry.

c   _____ I am happy at school, I would rather be at home!

d   I already ate one lolly _____ now I am going to eat another!

e   _____ I am always busy helping my family, I don't have time to play with my friends.

f   I ate lots of pink candyfloss _____ I went to the fair.

Different sentence types

1 Sort the following sentences into the table below by writing the letter (a–j) of the sentence into the relevant column.

a   Bo ran to school.

b   The computer broke so I lost all of my files.

c   Because I was cold, I put on a jumper.

d   Gideon watched football, so Marie went shopping.

e   The talk was very interesting as I expected.

f   Aiesha ate a cake.

g   Although he had lots of money, he was still miserable.

h   They waited for the plane but the plane was late.

i   When he had finished his breakfast, Chen realised he was late for work.

j   Beijing is the capital of China.

Simple	Compound	Complex

2 Write an example of each of the following types of sentence:

a   A command: _____

b   A statement: _____

c   A question: _____

d   An exclamation: _____

3 In these complex sentences, underline the following: connective in red, dependent clause in green and main clause in blue.

a   After the storm hit the town, there was lots of damage to buildings.

b   Although I had been invited, I chose not to go to the party.

Compound, complex or simple?

1 For each of the sentences below, tick whether it is a compound, complex or simple sentence. Use the notes on page 123 of the Learner's Book to help you.

	simple	compound	complex
When it was warm enough, Barid played in the sea.			
Jasmin paddled in the sea.			
I love spaghetti, but my brother loves lasagna.			
I walked to school, but the school was closed.			
Although I was tired, I kept running to the end of the race.			
Although it was dark, I went for a walk.			
I walked to school.			

2 Write your own example of a:

a   simple sentence

_____

_____

b   compound sentence

_____

_____

c   complex sentence

_____

_____

Verb tenses

1 Complete the verb table for the following verbs:

Verb	Past	Present	Future
to walk	I walked he/she/it walked we/you/they walked	I walk he/she/it _____ we/you walk	I _____ he/she/it will walk we/you
to work	I _____ he/she/it worked we/you/they _____	I _____ he/she/it works we/you work	I will work he/she/it _____ we/you _____
to smile	I smiled he/she/it _____ we/you/they _____	I smile he/she/it _____ we/you _____	I will smile he/she/it _____ we/you will smile

2 Using the verb table above, write the following sentences in the present tense (the first one has been done for you):

a   We _____ hard at school.

   We work hard at school

b   I _____ to school.

   _____

c   She _____ at people as they pass.

   _____

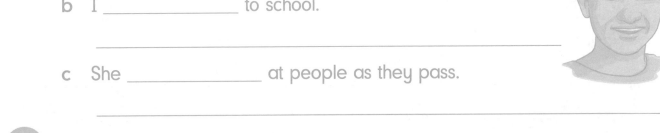

3 For each sentence below, identify the verb, tense and subject (the first one has been done for you):

a   He worked hard during the test.

Verb:	*worked*	Tense:	*past*	Subject:	*he*

b   You will walk to school tomorrow.

Verb:		Tense:		Subject:	

c   I smiled at the crowd.

Verb:		Tense:		Subject:	

Self-assessment
Unit 8
Changing stories into reports

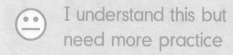

😊 I understand this well

😐 I understand this but need more practice

☹️ I don't understand this

Learning Objective	😊	😐	☹️
Reading			
I can read newspaper reports and think about how they engage the reader.			
I can identify key words and phrases to find the main point in a text.			
Writing			
I can use more powerful verbs in my writing.			
I can use different words to avoid repetition.			
I can investigate different tenses of verbs.			
I can use a wider range of connectives in my writing.			
I can write newspaper-style reports.			
I can make short notes from a text to help my writing.			
Speaking and listening			
I can understand the key points in an account and give my own comments.			

I need more help with ...

_____

_____

_____

_____

Unit 9 Imagery in poetry

Similes

Windigo

Hair like burnt moose moss
Head like a meat ball
Eyes like burning red ashes
Nose like a cow nose
Mouth like a flaming red hoop
Lips like red circles
Voice like an angry moose call
Breath like the dump
Teeth like sharpened swords
Ears like potatoes
Neck like a bear's neck
Body like a giant
Heart like an iceberg
Arms like stretchy telephone wires
Hand's like bears' claws
Legs like ice tunnels
Feet like wieners*
Toes like sliced apples.

By Sylvia Mark

*German sausages

1 Underline the similes in the poem.

2 Write alternatives for some of the similes in the poem, comparing the object with something different.

a   *Hair like golden straw.*

b   _____

c   _____

d   _____

e   _____

f   _____

3 Complete the following sentences using **as** or **like** to create a simile. Remember to make sure that the similes make sense.

a   Raindrops glistened _____

b   Houses towered above people _____

c   The giant's footsteps sounded _____

Alliteration

Autumn Gilt

The late September sunshine,
Lime green on the linden leaves,
Burns bronze on the slated roof-tops,
Yellow on the farmer's last sheaves.
It flares flame-like on the fire hydrant,
Is ebony on the blackbird's wing,
Blue beryl on the face of the ocean,
Glints gold on the bride's wedding ring.
A sparkling rainbow on the stained-glass window,
It's silver sheen on the kitchen sink,
The late September sunshine
Is a chameleon, I think.

By Valerie Bloom

1 Read the poem above and answer the following questions:

a Underline all the examples of alliteration used in the poem.

b Write your favourite example of alliteration and explain why you like it.

_____

_____

c The final two lines of the poem compares the sunshine to a chameleon. Explain what the poet means by this (look up the meaning of chameleon in a dictionary to help you).

_____

_____

d Find and write a word that shows the colour of the sun on the blackbird's wing.

_____

e Give a reason why you think the colours on the stained glass window are described as a rainbow?

_____

_____

Similes and alliteration

1 For each of the words shown in the table write:
a   a simile that could be used to describe it.
b   an alliterative phrase that could be used.

An example has been done for you.

	Simile	Alliteration
Ant	*as tiny as a sunflower seed*	*active ants...*
Ball		
Cheetah		
Baby		
Tree		
Car		
Cheese		
Sky		
Spaghetti		
Aeroplane		

Rhyming in poetry

Poem 1

Last night I had a healthy meal,
The yams were really great,
I even ate the carrots
That took up half my plate.

The fish was quite delicious,
And the rice and peas divine,
The sauce was hot and burned
my mouth,
But the cabbage tasted fine.

Poem 2

Where did all the dodos go?
That's something only dodos know,
But finding out's no easy task.
There are no dodos left to ask.

1 For poems 1 and 2:

 a Underline the words that rhyme in different colours (For example, blue for two words that rhyme, red for two other words that rhyme).

 b Identify the rhyming pattern:

 Poem 1: _____

 Poem 2: _____

2 Which is your favourite of the two poems and why?

 My favourite poem is _____

 because _____

 _____

3 a What did the poet dislike eating in poem 1?

 _____

 b Why can't we ask the dodos where they have gone?

 _____

Rhyming schemes

1 Write three rhyming words for each noun in the table below.

Noun	Word 1	Word 2	Word 3
root	*boot*	*loot*	*hoot*
boat			
sun			
tree			

2 Using the words above (or others that rhyme), complete each of these poems, making sure that you follow the rhyme scheme shown.

a   Rhyme scheme: AABB

I paddled my boat

_____

Gleaming in the sun

_____

b   Rhyme scheme: ABAB

I looked down at the root

I looked up at the tree

_____

_____

c   Rhyme scheme: ABCB

I glanced up at the sun

And down at the boat

_____

_____

Onomatopoeia

1 Design an exciting poster, using each of the words listed in the box to show the sound they make.

For example, the word *hiss* might be small and long. For example, *H i s s* to show the long, quiet sound that it makes.

My poster:

> Words to include in your poster:
> crackle, creak, crunch, slurp, puff, moo, ring

Figurative language features

1 Find the words from the box and circle them in the wordsearch.

a	h	y	y	r	j	v	h	g	e	a	o
h	l	w	x	r	n	u	m	s	b	n	m
s	l	l	f	l	e	v	f	n	o	w	x
m	u	b	i	i	a	g	s	m	w	l	k
q	y	r	q	t	y	t	a	t	i	e	x
g	i	q	a	r	e	t	a	m	v	l	v
n	m	v	t	s	o	r	k	q	i	i	g
f	b	e	j	p	e	m	a	l	a	m	h
a	o	g	o	i	i	f	w	t	i	i	y
p	v	e	r	h	y	m	e	b	i	s	w
l	i	g	c	a	k	m	h	z	z	o	r
a	e	v	i	t	a	r	u	g	i	f	n

alliteration
figurative
imagery
onomatopoeia
poetry
rhyme
simile

2 Match each word to its definition by drawing lines between them.

alliteration	Words that sound like the sound they are describing
onomatopoeia	Language that creates a visual image for the reader
simile	When two words sound the same or have the same sound endings.
imagery	The same sound or letter at the beginning of adjacent words
rhyme	when one thing is compared to another to improve description

Types of language

1   a   Write 3 sentences using a simile in each:

    i   _____

    ii   _____

    iii   _____

  b   Write 3 different alliterative phrases:

    i   _____

    ii   _____

    iii   _____

  c   Write 3 examples of onomatopoeic words:

    i   _____

    ii   _____

    iii   _____

2   Explain how figurative language creates mood.

_____

_____

3   Match these sentences to the type of figurative language used.

She saw the stormy sea.	onomatopoeia
The car drove as fast as a rocket.	rhyme
Crash!	alliteration
It is fine to dine.	simile

Self-assessment
Unit 9
Imagery in poetry

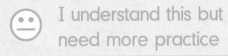 😊 I understand this well

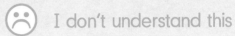 😐 I understand this but need more practice

😞 I don't understand this

Learning Objective	😊	😐	😞
Reading			
I know what onomatopoeia means.			
I understand how figurative language can be used to create mood.			
I can explain how imagery and figurative language can impact poetry.			
Writing			
I can build words from other words with similar meanings.			
I can re-read my own writing to check punctuation and grammar.			
I can choose and compare words to strengthen the impact of my writing.			
I can use similes in my writing.			
I can use alliteration in my writing.			
Speaking and listening			
I can adapt the pace and volume of my speech when performing to an audience.			

 I need more help with ...

The Publishers would like to thank the following for permission to reproduce copyright material:

Acknowledgements

p13, from **Escape from Pompeii** *by Christina Balit, published by Frances Lincoln Ltd copyright © 2005, reproduced by permission of Frances Lincoln Ltd; p19,* **Listen** *by Telcine Turner by permission of the author, Telcine Turner; p63, 65 extracts from* **The Works 4** *compiled by Gaby Morgan and Pie Corbett (published by Macmillan) copyright © the individual authors; p20,* **Humming Bird** *by DH Lawrence (d.1930); p22, from* **Silly Verses for Kids** *by Spike Milligan (published by Puffin Books Ltd); p32, from* **Harry's Mad** *by Dick King-Smith (published by Puffin Books Ltd); p35, from* **Charlie and the Chocolate Factory** *by Roald Dahl, published by Jonathan Cape Ltd and Penguin Books Ltd and reproduced by permission; p51, from* **Harry Potter and the Philosopher's Stone** *by J.K. Rowling,* copyright © J.K. Rowling 1997 *(published by Bloomsbury); p62,* **Windigo** *by Sylvia Marks; p65,* **Romain's Healthy Meal** *from Caribbean Comprehension: an integrated, skills-based approach, published by Hodder Education; p65, poem 2 by Rosie Kent.*

Every effort has been made to trace all copyright holders, but if any have been inadvertently overlooked the Publishers will be pleased to make the necessary arrangements at the first opportunity.

Although every effort has been made to ensure that website addresses are correct at time of going to press, Hodder Education cannot be held responsible for the content of any website mentioned in this book. It is sometimes possible to find a relocated web page by typing in the address of the home page for a website in the URL window of your browser.

Hachette Livre UK's policy is to use papers that are natural, renewable and recyclable products and made from wood grown in sustainable forests. The logging and manufacturing processes are expected to conform to the environmental regulations of the country of origin.

Orders: please contact Bookpoint Ltd, 130 Milton Park, Abingdon, Oxon OX14 4SB.
Telephone: +44 (0)1235 827720. Fax: +44 (0)1235 400454. Lines are open 9.00 a.m.–5.00 p.m., Monday to Saturday, with a 24-hour message answering service. Visit our website at www.hoddereducation.com

© Sarah Snashall 2014
First published in 2014 by
Hodder Education,
An Hachette UK Company
Carmelite House
50 Victoria Embankment
London EC4Y 0DZ

Impression number   10 9 8 7
Year   2019 2018 2017

Cover illustration by Sandy Lightley
Illustrations by Marleen Visser
Typeset in Swissforall 14pt
Printed in Great Britain by Hobbs the Printers, Totton, Hampshire

A catalogue record for this title is available from the British Library

ISBN 978 1471 830280

Cambridge Primary

Hodder Cambridge Primary
English
Stage 4

Hodder Cambridge Primary English is a complete English course supporting the Cambridge Primary English curriculum framework. The books have been written by experienced primary practitioners specifically for Cambridge Primary.

Each unit of work is based on a reading genre within fiction, non-fiction or poetry. The activities cover the objectives from all areas of the Cambridge Primary English curriculum framework: *Reading, Writing* and *Speaking and listening*. The Workbook supports the activities in the Learner's Book and Teacher's Pack.

Each Workbook includes:

- additional activities linked to the Learner's Book, providing further practice to consolidate the objectives
- a learner-friendly self-assessment page at the end of each unit.

The series consists of a Learner's Book, Teacher's Pack and Workbook for each Cambridge Primary stage. Books in the **Hodder Cambridge Primary English** series:

	Learner's Books	Teacher's Packs	Workbooks
Stage 1 (ages 5–6)	9781471831003	9781471831010	9781471831027
Stage 2 (ages 6–7)	9781471830211	9781471830259	9781471830242
Stage 3 (ages 7–8)	9781471830976	9781471830983	9781471830990
Stage 4 (ages 8–9)	9781471830266	9781471830273	9781471830280
Stage 5 (ages 9–10)	9781471830761	9781471830952	9781471830969
Stage 6 (ages 10–11)	9781471830204	9781471830228	9781471830235

Working with 25 YEARS Cambridge International Examinations

For 25 years we have been trusted by Cambridge schools around the world to provide quality support for teaching and learning. For this reason we have been selected by Cambridge International Examinations as an official publisher of endorsed material for their syllabuses.

This resource is endorsed by Cambridge International Examinations

✓ Provides learner support as part of a set of resources for the Cambridge Primary English curriculum framework from 2018

✓ Has passed Cambridge's rigorous quality-assurance process

✓ Developed by subject experts

✓ For Cambridge schools worldwide

HODDER EDUCATION
www.hoddereducation.com

ISBN 978-1-471-83028-0